PRAISE FOR LORENZO SANFORD

Lorenzo Sanford

"Any good astrologer can read and interpret symbols. However, what makes Lorenzo an awfully good astrologer is his innate ability to understand people. This is a gift he was born with and has worked to perfect. He has been reading my charts for the past 30 years and rarely has he not been spot on. In fact, notwithstanding his extraordinary musicianship, understanding human beings and communicating such with wisdom, insight, and empathy is his calling."

— Dr. Jasmine Williams,
PROFESSOR OF HISTORY, TEXAS

"I WAS BLESSED TO RECEIVE an astrological reading from Lorenzo. He took the time to explain and ensure understanding, with compassion and empathy. As he progressed through the reading and elucidated what he saw in my chart, his level of expertise became immediately evident. He was reading my life and experiences! Lorenzo demonstrated true commitment and concern for me as a client. I have already recommended his services to others and would do so again and again."

— Amobiye Nkromah,
LICENSED PSYCHOTHERAPIST, PENNSYLVANIA

"**LORENZO'S READING WAS INSTRUMENTAL** in helping guide me in a pivotal transition point in my life. I could feel this coming up and he verified my feelings using the stars. His style of incorporating conversation into the reading was very reassuring. On our first meeting, we went very deep! I was comfortable doing so due to Lorenzo's caring nature."

— Lisa Taylor, Coach, Shamanic Healer,
MEDITATION FACILITATOR, CALIFORNIA

"**LORENZO IS GIFTED!** When he confirmed what has been living in my spirit, my soul felt in full harmony and exhaled with every word that was in alignment with my entire being. My astrological reading based on my life's purpose was refreshing and my spirit's call to action! I am full on ready to FULLY walk in my calling! I feel incredibly blessed by my experience and I courageously walk in the purpose of which I Am..."

— TAJ, Entrepreneur,
SPIRITUAL LIFE COACH, NEW YORK

"**LORENZO QUITE LITERALLY BLEW MY MIND!** I've been getting readings from astrologers and numerologists for years now and this was by far my most accurate and life-changing reading. I'm still speechless at the relevance of what he's able to perceive. Also, his spiritual guidance on how to use the astrological information for tangible shifts in my life was invaluable. Lorenzo has a unique and special gift!"

— Elphia Paul,
CELEBRITY PRIVATE CHEF & WHOLISTIC WELLNESS ADVISOR, ST. LUCIA

The Beautiful Logic of Astrology

**YOUR GUIDE TO UNDERSTANDING
THE FUNDAMENTAL LANGUAGE OF THE STARS**

LORENZO SANFORD

ASTRO-LOGIC

Cover and illustrations by Vivian McDuffie, © 2021, pages 40, 44, 48, 52, 56, 60, 64, 68, 72, 76, 80, and 84

Art direction, design and layout: Scott Wood

For permission requests, write to the publisher, **Attention: Permissions Coordinator,** at **INFO@ASTROLOGICASTROLOGY.COM**

ACKNOWLEDGMENTS

I must give my deepest gratitude to those who supported me throughout this process and in the process of completing this project. To the magical Gemini, Candace Apple, who opened the doors of her mystical playground, the Phoenix and Dragon Bookstore, and invited me in to accept my astrological calling and to play. To Capricorn Tony Lamair Burks II, EdD, whose encouragement instilled confidence in me to pursue this and who provided the early foundational structures that allowed me to translate my knowledge into this book. To my writing coach, Laurie Baum, who gently yet firmly brought me back down to Earth, when I would, in my true Libran nature, escape into warm and fuzzy ideas that had not yet matured into concrete usefulness. To my friend and advisor, Amobiye Nkromah, who's Cancer Sun and ascendant energy always gave me safe harbor when I worried. To Chantel Hampton, my brilliant Libra branding savant, for being both deeply invested in and creatively inspired to help my astrology business be the best it can possibly be. Finally, to my beautiful, determined and soulful Sagittarian wife, Dorian McDuffie, who would not let me improvise and who provided outlines for each chapter, which focused my teaching of this material, making it more accessible and attainable for my students (and for me)!

TO ROYETTA

MY UNWAVERING MOTHER,

MY TRUEST FOUNDATION,

IT ALL BEGAN WITH YOU,

LITERALLY AND

FIGURATIVELY.

CONTENTS

FORWARD X

INTRODUCTION XII

OVERVIEW XVI

FIRST THOUGHTS XVIII

PART I: The Signs as Energy Archetypes 19

PART 2: The Planets 89

PART 3: The Houses 99

PART 4: The Aspects 109

PART 5: Putting It All Together 115

ABOUT THE AUTHOR 122

FORWARD

Using astrology to guide one's life is not a new concept. More than once in your life you've likely consulted the stars for guidance—probably by checking your horoscope. Many of us know our zodiac (Sun) sign—the sign we were "born under," but the sky—the stars, planets and other celestial bodies—can tell us so much more about who we are, who we can become, and how we relate to one another and the world. We just have to know the language it speaks. Once you have that powerful knowledge, you'll see that your life story is literally in the stars.

Your natal chart is a map of the sky at the moment of your birth. It shows the positions of the planets and their relationship to one another at the time you took your first breath. It is a map unique to you. Just like reading a road map provides clarity to your travel, your birth map provides clarity to your life. When you understand the significance of the planets, their placements and how they "talk" to one another, you will be able to read your life's journey; past, present and future. My personal experience with reading my natal chart began with Lorenzo Sanford as my guide—and the journey made me laugh, cry and experience sheer awe at what it revealed. I gained insight and answered questions to the "whys" that have plagued me for years. The impact of Lorenzo's teaching me this material was profound. There is something humbling, moving and deeply enriching that comes from being able to make meaning of your story as it was designed to be. Yet, it's all right there in the natal chart.

As Lorenzo will show you with *The Beautiful Logic of Astrology*, astrology is a fun and fascinating study. It is intricate, multi-layered and within it you can discover, uncover, reveal, and heal. Astrology opens the door to new learning experiences for all aspects of life. It can help you find answers, make sense of chaos and even determine life events!

My hope for you is that you will find this book inspiring; that you will want to learn more about astrology and its multiple components and in the process discover yourself. To say that you will begin to see the world differently is an understatement. Your life perspective will become broader and more meaningful, and you will always have a source for answers to your questions.

And this is just the beginning....

Valerie Edwards

VALERIE EDWARDS, LPC
Marietta, Georgia
February, 2021

INTRODUCTION

Astrology is a language that employs many unique symbols. When properly understood, these symbols will speak to you about the universe you inhabit. The language it speaks is amazing and wonderful! Astrology is the voice of the rhythm and character of the most profound dimensions of life.

The most important thing that you need to understand about astrology is that it is based on thousands of years of observation, of human temperament and personality. Astrology is older than religion (most religions have elements derived from astrology) and it represents humanity's search for understanding the reasons we act the way that we do.

The basic tenet of astrology is, "as it is above, so it is below." The second part of this statement is, "the within is as the without" ("as" is the keyword here). The meaning that we derive from these primary pillars of astrology is that you become an agent of the time into which you are born. When astrologers construct your birth chart, we calculate for that day and for the exact time and location of your birth. This is vital and necessary because your birth chart reveals that when you came out of your mother's womb, when your umbilical cord was cut, when you took your first breath and cried, you started vibrating to the rhythm and the character of the universe. By character, we mean discernible qualities of energy that reverberated in the world at that time. You absorbed the qualities of that specific time and became separate from your mother as a living being; and one who experienced life through energies transmitted by the umbilical cord. Everything that previously poured into you came from her. But then the cord was cut ... and you started vibrating to the energy of that time. That is significant because it emphatically states that you are different from everyone else, based upon the moment of your birth.

This is the greatest value of astrology—it tells you who you are as a unique energetic being in this world. If you acknowledge this at a deep level, there is no need to ever want or try to be like anyone else. Thus, what is normally considered a trite cliché turns out to be insurmountably true: in all your perfect imperfections, you are not designed to be anyone else in the world but you! In fact, according to astrological theory, the specifics of an individual birth chart are not repeated for 26,000 years!

The purpose of this guidebook is to give you a firm grasp of the fundamentals of astrology. It is designed to help you understand the symbols of your unique energy patterns, through astrological theory and your own observations of what these theories look like in real life. As your understanding of fundamental astrological theory grows, (through memorizing the meanings of the planets, signs, houses and aspects), you will be equipped to transform the quality and experience of your life. You may also lay the foundation for becoming a great astrologer!

If you are open to learning the specific methods of interpreting astrological symbolism, you can learn about every dimension of human aspiration and endeavor. These dimensions include desire, empathy, inspiration, ambition, mental acuity, attraction, anger, fear, spiritual transformation, and more. There is no longer any question of whether astrological language can offer a deeper understanding of the human experience. The only question is, "how fluent will you become in understanding and speaking this rich language?"

The intent of this guidebook is to offer a pathway to anyone who wants to learn to interpret the meanings and messages expressed by our universe. This book will guide you in the discovery of your voice and purpose. It will also help you understand the people closest to you.

The journey of a lifetime begins here, where foundational astrological tools are introduced and explained in an easy-to-read, step-by-step approach. May your understanding of these symbols and the universal energies they represent, bring you peace, insight and illumination, and be reflected in your life experiences.

Namaste,

Lorenzo A. Sanford, III

ASTRO-LOGIC

OVERVIEW:
FUNDAMENTALS OF ASTROLOGY

There are four principal factors in the astrological system: planets, signs, houses and aspects. Learning the basic dimensions of each of these four primary factors will give you self-understanding and purposeful comprehension of others.

Planets express the "what" of any astrological equation. What urge is wanting to express itself? The signs show how. How are the planets acting out their urges; are they assertive, passive, moody, practical? The houses show where. Where will the planets act out their urges? The aspects show the ease or difficulty planets will have expressing their urges and what other planets help or hinder their energy flow.

Profound and simple at the same time. But not easy. Astrology mirrors life and everyone over the age of three knows that life is challenging. To put it generously, life is nuanced! Therefore, you're going to have to invest some time and study to become proficient at reading and understanding astrology for yourself or for others.

This is because astrological symbolism is only a map. It happens to be a great map that is without equal in the world of human knowledge. Still, maps can never equal the experience of the journey. Even high-tech digital maps that give you every detail of what is likely to be on your path cannot give you a lived experience. The astrological system is a map of living processes. Life (and your human family) must be experienced with all aspects of your being. It is never enough to theorize, as theory is merely a fraction of the whole truth. So, by all means, do follow the maps. But please, know that if you are to arrive at any worthwhile astrological destination, which is to say any deep understanding of yourself and others, it will require you to explore and live in the actual territory. This system is essentially a study of human consciousness. To approach and understand it, you will need tools. This book will serve that purpose. The material presented here, combined with the compassion of your heart and the intuitive powers of your mind, body and spirit, will make this a journey well worth taking.

FIRST THOUGHTS

USE ANY OF THESE PROMPTS TO
TRIGGER YOUR IMMEDIATE THOUGHTS:

I have always felt that astrology...

I knew astrology would be a part of my world when...

I have wondered if astrology...

I think astrology is...

I have feared that astrology...

ASTRO LOGIC

Part I
THE ASTROLOGICAL SIGNS: ENERGY ARCHETYPES

Think about the behavior of someone close to you. Ask yourself the question, "How is this person unlike anyone else I know?"

Consider a few examples of behaviors that describe their unique characteristics.

EVERYONE knows someone who stands out like no one else. But what's true is that we all stand out. The astrological factor that most describes our uniqueness is found in the Zodiac signs. You love your Leo uncle because he is the guy who tells the stories of his prowess, "back in the day," and it could be anything from his achievements on an athletic field, or his achievements with the ladies. One thing is certain, he absolutely was the man. Whether or not you roll your eyes in disbelief, or you or someone else in the family sit in rapt attention to his glorious details, your uncle is displaying a quintessential Leo personality characteristic. It's all about him!

Then there is the person who, when they are right, they are right and everyone else is wrong. Which astrological sign do you think represents this characteristic best? Is it your Aquarius brother, who, while it is clear he tends to be correct 80 percent of the time, still will not acknowledge the 20 percent of the time that he is wrong, because his ego cannot ever admit that he is sometimes simply ordinary and not the world's only genius?

What about the person who seems to know everyone's business in the neighborhood, whose life only has meaning in the context of her "sharing" what she believes to be the facts of someone else's life predicament. Is this neighborhood gossip coincidently born in late May or the first few weeks in June? Why is it so amazing that astrology books describe Gemini characteristics that fit your neighbor to a T?

We are having fun with these vignettes. Yet, there is an uncanny correlation between the behaviors that the astrological signs describe and the ways people we know act. My favorite way of making sense of these patterns that our friends and loved ones embody is to use examples from nature. There are themes that repeat in nature that also show up in human conduct. Let's take a look at the characteristics of one sign from each of the four seasons.

Every spring, new life emerges. After winter, when the grass turns green, or when tulips begin to bloom, nature is telling us in dramatic fashion that life is renewing itself again. And that bright, bold, green grass has no idea that any other reality existed before. It only knows that it is here and it's time for the fun to begin. Isn't that just like your experience of your Aries friends?

How soul warming does it feel to know that, in June, there will be a long period when you will be bathed in light; that the Sun will envelop you every day and make you feel lovingly protected from the harshness of cold days past? Have you ever met a Cancer person who did not make you feel safe and cared for like that?

Consider the feeling of life after a wonderful but blistering summer, when the weather finds a middle ground between hot and cold and the air is sweet. The time of year when you can see nature's beauty and its intelligence, in the leaves that begin to turn from green to varying hues of amber, bronze and golden honey. Does this not resemble the effortless way your Libra friends always seem to look amazing and yet never have to sweat for it?

Then think of what life feels like in January, when it sometimes seems that the Earth is unresponsive. Yet, if we are honest, we also come to accept that there is wisdom in nature's removing all the pomp and pageantry, while essential processes are being maintained beneath the cold surface. Our Capricorn friends are the perfect embodiment of this no nonsense but always productive season of life.

If you look closely at nature, you will find that there are characteristics that perfectly reflect attitudes and behaviors of all living beings. The astrological signs are symbolic scripts, myths that emerged from thousands of years of human observation, passed down to us for our growth. You do not have to accept every description of the astrological signs that you read. Indeed, be alert and find descriptions of your own. However, understand that humans still exist as a part of nature. Therefore, we will always be connected to its vast purposes and manifestations.

Think about the time of year someone close to you was born. How does this person reflect or portray the energy of that season? Use your imagination, be open to any characteristics that are very apparent, then simply personify them. Have fun with this exercise. There are no absolute answers, right or wrong. Hopefully you can connect living people with energy that is observable in nature. After you do this, explore how your descriptions correlate to descriptions of their Sun sign.

THE ELEMENTS

As energy archetypes, the 12 zodiac signs also correlate with the basic composition of all living matter:

Fire – heat

Earth – solids

Air – gases

Water – liquids

In astrology we are concerned with the way these energy archetypes function as the four primary psychological temperaments that all humans possess. Within each group of temperaments there are three astrological signs:

FIRE SIGNS:
ARIES, LEO, SAGITTARIUS

Fire represents the principle of action. People born under fire signs are noted for their straightforward and enthusiastic natures. They tend to be excited about life and will create opportunities instead of waiting for life to open opportunities to them. They can also be generous, because they have an innate faith that there is always enough supply to meet life's demands.

EARTH SIGNS:
TAURUS, VIRGO, CAPRICORN

Earth represents the principle of stability. People born under earth signs are noted for being reliable and consistent. They tend to be deliberate and methodical and thus do not like to be rushed. Because they are consummate planners, the achievements that are attributed to them will be long lasting.

AIR SIGNS:
GEMINI, LIBRA, AQUARIUS

Air represents the principle of thought. People born under air signs act on everything according to their sense of logic. They weigh their life options in terms of what is most reasonable. They tend to need a lot of space, as they are always processing a great deal of information in and through their minds. They are the great communicators of the zodiac.

WATER SIGNS:
CANCER, SCORPIO, PISCES

Water represents the principle of emotion. People born under the element of water are very sensitive to the undercurrents of energy around them. They can feel the "vibe" in a room without anyone having to tell them anything. This trait also makes them aware of what other people are experiencing. They are the empaths of the zodiac. They respond to life's changes with fluidity and have an extraordinary ability to demonstrate tenderness, affection and caring to those in need.

EARTH
practical

FIRE
dynamic

WATER
emotional

AIR
logical

AIR
logical

WATER
emotional

EARTH
practical

FIRE
dynamic

FIRE
dynamic

EARTH
practical

AIR
logical

WATER
emotional

THE MODALITIES

While each of the four elements describes a specific temperament, there is another layer of symbolism that gives greater nuance and complexity to the astrological language. The 12 Zodiac signs can be divided into three categories that operate in predictable ways: cardinal (initiating), fixed (stable) and mutable (changeable). They represent the basic way that these groups of signs operate.

CARDINAL SIGNS:
ARIES, CANCER, LIBRA, CAPRICORN

FIXED SIGNS:
TAURUS, LEO, SCORPIO, AQUARIUS

MUTABLE SIGNS:
GEMINI, VIRGO, SAGITTARIUS, PISCES

A good way to understand the modalities is to again use the model of the changing seasons. The cardinal signs represent the first signs of each of nature's four seasons. Aries, the cardinal fire sign, is the energy that initiates spring. Cancer, the cardinal water sign, is the energy that initiates summer. Libra, the cardinal air sign, is the energy that initiates fall. Capricorn, the cardinal earth sign, is the energy that initiates winter. Each of these periods in nature brings a demonstrable change of

seasonal conditions; one that leads the way for the quality of the climate to follow. Similarly, each of the cardinal signs brings a strong focus on the psychological element (action, stability, thought, feeling) to which it belongs.

Remember, we are describing cycles in nature as a way of describing psychological traits. After the intense activity of the beginning of each new season, inevitably nature reaches a state of calm and stability. Likewise in astrology, cardinal signs give way to fixed signs. The fixed signs stabilize and maintain what was begun in the cardinal period. In springtime Taurus represents the calm earth that is ready to receive seeds planted in stable soil, in the northern hemisphere. In late July, Leo represents the dramatic and unyielding summer heat. In the fall, Scorpio represents the once beautiful leaves that have finished their journey for the year and are giving way to a profound period of transformation. Finally, in late January, Aquarius establishes the ruthlessly cold weather, that makes it known to all that nature has its own unique process that cannot be changed—no matter how much some wish for a more comfortable experience.

The stable periods in nature always evolve and eventually transition. Similarly, the mutable signs, though not dramatically as the other modalities, facilitate natural and needed change. Gemini, Virgo, Sagittarius, Pisces and their corresponding times of year, consistently reveal that nothing remains constant and all must absorb new information in order to shift perspective and potentially become more than they were before.

To summarize, the modalities describe the natural ways humanity functions. All things considered, the signs, in their distinct elements and modalities, illuminate living processes. In human consciousness, as in nature, awareness of certain types of energy causes growth and change. The initial burst of new life (or awareness) eventually evolves into other seasons. All of humanity engages in these primary processes: initiate, stabilize and transition to the next cycle of development. Astrology provides powerful symbols that systematically translate the symbiotic connection between man and nature.

THE MODALITIES

CARDINAL

Represents action. Each sign of the cardinal modality has the ability to lead. (Cardinal Signs: Aries, Cancer, Libra, Capricorn)

FIXED

After an initiation of energy, a sign of fixed quality stabilizes the situation. The fixed modality finds it hard to change and a person with this quality will usually be confidently set in their ways. (Fixed Signs: Taurus, Leo, Scorpio, Aquarius)

MUTABLE

People born under mutable signs see life from many perspectives. They are flexible and enjoy movement and change. They represent the need to transition, so there may be touch of unpredictability in their natures. (Mutable Signs: Gemini, Virgo, Sagittarius, Pisces)

UNDERSTANDING THE STRUCTURE OF THE BIRTH CHART

The "ascendant" or "first house" of the 12 houses in the zodiac wheel, is based upon the moment of birth and the sign of the zodiac that was rising over the eastern horizon at the moment of your first breath. A natal astrology chart is a map of the positions of the planets at the moment and location of birth (based on time and space).

In the illustrated wheel on the following page, the symbols of the zodiac signs are displayed around the perimeter of the zodiacal wheel. Astrology was originally conceived as an agricultural system. The ancients knew to plant the seeds for new crops when the constellation of Aries was rising at dawn. Each subsequent constellation represented a new energy gracing the planet. The cycle of signs continues consecutively until the land lays fallow at the last sign of the zodiac, Pisces.

The beginning sign of each person's chart (the ascendant) is determined by your time and place of birth. Each of the 12 astrological signs are contained in every chart. Everyone has 12 signs in their chart, but in different zodiac locations around the 360° wheel.

Each of the planets in different constellations around the 360° wheel represent various psychological drives, progressing from the simple desire to live and thrive in the first sign, Aries, to the desire to merge with Spirit in the 12th sign, Pisces.

CREATING YOUR BIRTH CHART

You can go to my website to request your free birth chart: www.astrologicastrology.com, all you need is your birth date (month/day/year), location (city/state) and your birth time. On the bottom of the home page click the "Birth Chart" link and insert the information requested. Do your best to make sure that your birth time is correct. It is possible to get an accurate birth time from your state, or from the hospital you were born in. If needed, take the extra time to find out your accurate data. It will make your chart precise. However, if you can't locate your exact birth time, we can still give you a chart with the major planet information, especially your natal Sun and Moon.

Twelve astrological compartments called houses comprise the 360° wheel. The astrological houses represent where the planetary drives play out. The houses represent areas of life that everyone has in common. Your chart is colored by the zodiac sign influencing each particular house, again, based upon the time and place of your birth.

The order of the houses remains the same, numbered from One to 12. The first house is considered to be the strongest house in the chart. This house describes your physical appearance and your primary approach to life.

When planets are placed in any of the 12 houses, this indicates that certain energies are operating in very defined areas of life. The planets describe which psychological drive is being expressed. The signs describe how energy is

THE ASTROLOGICAL SIGNS: ENERGY ARCHETYPES

being expressed. The houses point to where the energy is being directed. The planet, the sign and the house must be considered together to have a full view of the energy the chart describes. To view the complete 360° chart may at first seem confusing. However, if it is seen as a cycle of experiences that progresses, it facilitates understanding all of life's circumstances as related experiences.

DEGREES

There are 30° in each of the 12 signs, comprising a 360° circle. The degrees are counted beginning at 0° and ending at 29°. The degrees roughly approximate the movement of the Sun through the sky as it passes through each constellation. So, for example, on March 20th each year the Sun is at 0° of Aries. On March 30th, the Sun is at 10° of Aries and on April 10th, the Sun is at 20° of Aries. By April 20th, the Sun has passed through 29° of Aries and is now at 0° of Taurus.

When reading a chart (see page 118), sign degrees are represented by the number that precedes the symbol for each sign on the outer perimeter (section one of the chart wheel). The degree indicates where the planet is located within the spectrum of the sign. The astrological wheel is 360°. Each sign contains 30° — (12 signs x 30° = 360°).

Planetary positions also are calculated by degrees. The degree indicates where a planet is located within a sign. Planets can only fall into one of the 30 degrees of each sign. The planetary degrees are represented by the number located in section two (see page 118) of the zodiac wheel next to the planetary glyph. You will see this when reading the chart starting from the outside of the circle, moving in.

Additionally, please note that there are 60 minutes in each degree. While it is not necessary for you to delve deeply into this point at this stage of your journey, it is valuable to know the meaning of the number following the sign glyph on the innermost rim of the zodiac wheel.

The planets and signs determine HOW energy is expressed and the houses point to WHERE the energy is expressed. All planets act through the sign AND the house they are located in. Both the sign and the house must be considered together.

THE ASTROLOGICAL "I" STATEMENTS

The following "I" statements are meant to describe the energy of the signs with an identifying word. Take a moment to consider responses to these questions: What is the "I" statement like in action in the real world? If a person is a manifestation of their "I" statement, what would that be or look like at home? At work? In relationships?

ARIES: "I am"

TAURUS: "I have"

GEMINI: "I think"

CANCER: "I feel"

LEO: "I shine"

VIRGO: "I critique"

LIBRA: "I balance"

SCORPIO: "I regenerate"

SAGITTARIUS: "I explore"

CAPRICORN: "I use"

AQUARIUS: "I know"

PISCES: "I believe"

Aries

I AM

THERE ARE TWO TYPES OF ARIES: the ones who totally shun social media and the ones who post everything that comes to their mind, regardless of how personal it may be. Believe it or not both types share a common motivation. Aries is ruled by the planet Mars. Many people know the symbol of Mars because it has come to represent masculinity. In ancient myths Mars was the god of war and much of his symbolism in astrology comes from those sources. The common theme in war and masculinity is aggression. If that word is troublesome, let's use the word bold. This gets us closer to the Aries essence, for they simply have no fear. They don't even have the inner mechanisms for fear based thinking. All they know is that "I am here, now let's go!"

How can anyone avoid social media? Who dares to live a life that doesn't acknowledge the influence of the all important "they?" Those who share our interests and want to know what's going on in our lives. Those who are in our fields of endeavor and may need to be reminded that we have something valuable to contribute to the field. Even those who are our family members. Who can ignore all of that peer pressure and decide that, "I don't care about that?" "I don't need that?" "Whats in it for me?" Who is that bold? Some Aries people.

On the other hand, what type of person puts everything they do, from their day at the hair salon, the type of food they eat, and every single event connected to their work and career, no matter how intimate (or boring), on social media? Who is bold enough to put it all out there, as if to say, "What? I'm in it for me" – an Aries.

If it's not clear to you yet, Aries people don't care what you think of them. They don't give a flying pluck if you like them. They could care less if you never acknowledge them, because they acknowledge themselves. Aries are courageous. They are not afraid to stand out from the crowd. In fact, they prefer it. They have a burning need to walk their own path, not one blazed by someone else. Aries is a cardinal fire sign, making them natural born leaders. As in the case of a dear friend of mine, who held a high profile position as a musician in the band of one of the biggest stars in music. She could have made tons of money and had notoriety and access to different channels of influence for years to come. But, being an Aries, she almost had no choice. Her ruling planet Mars, the fearless and bold instigator in her soul, would not allow her to stay long. She had her own plans. She walked. She is still doing her thing. She is an Aries.

ARIES
MARCH 21 – APRIL 20

ELEMENT	MODALITY	ASSOCIATED HOUSE	PLANET
Fire	Cardinal	1ST • Self	Mars

- Rules the head and leads with the head
- Initiates new beginnings
- Likes to be the first, has a competitive nature
- Can be impulsive, taking action before thorough consideration
- Tends to be impatient, aggressive
- Is instinctively brave and unafraid of risk
- Possesses youthful strength and energy, regardless of age

Taurus

I HAVE

DUKE ELLINGTON, ONE OF THE MOST IMPORTANT composers of all time, and Stevie Wonder, a musical giant whose work bridges both the 20th and 21st centuries, were born under the earth sign of Taurus. What is striking about these two musicians is their staying power, both have careers that lasted longer than most artists in their time. Tauruses can remain focused on whatever they care about until the proverbial cows come home. They just don't quit. And why should they? When is the right time to release something that you have nurtured, built, or created? If you are asking a Taurus person this question, the answer will be a resounding, "NEVER."

Maybe you disagree. But be careful, if you dare tell a Taurus person that their way is not the only way. Stevie Wonder has a song called "Superwoman," in which he plaintively states, "Mary wants to be a superwoman and try to boss the bull around, but does she really think she'll get by with a dream?" Then he answered that question in the next lyric, saying, "My woman wants to be a superwoman and I just had to say good-bye." What's so intriguing about this story is how beautiful the song is, for someone who is essentially saying, no matter how strong, ambitious or capable you are, If you push me, I will simply leave you." Is this a sign of someone who could be considered myopic? A Taurus person won't even hear the question, why are we even talking about this? Because, if you are in relationship with a Taurus man, woman or child, once they dig in and decide on a course of action, you need to know that you will rarely change their mind. End of story. I should add that there is absolutely no malice involved when Taurus people settle into their positions. They have a natural innocence with everything they do.

But they will provide money, food, sex and security for you! They will bring Venus energy, which means pleasure. While they won't change for you, they will be such amazing anchors of stability in your life, maybe its not such a bad compromise. Let's not ask Aquarians, Leos or Scorpios about this. Venus as the ruling planet for Taurus, asks that something meaningful, beautiful and lasting be built. Often what they build is made with their own hands. Once something has been conceived, planted and grown, whether it be a business, a relationship or a creative project, Tauruses manage and remain in possession of what they begin. Yes, they can resist change in a way that is reminiscent of a child throwing a tantrum. Yes, they may overindulge in various sensual pleasures. Yes, they may keep the money, house, company, relationship, under tight wraps. But somebody has to stay the course. It might as well be someone who is calm, creative, patient, supportive and resilient. It might as well be your Taurus family member or friend. When Duke Ellington wrote the hit song, "It Don't Mean A Thing If It Ain't Got That Swing," undoubtedly he was talking about a quality of enduring magic, a rhythm that you can count on to keep you feeling like life is flowing your way. This is pure Taurus symbolism, representing people who know how to maintain a good thing.

TAURUS
APRIL 21 – MAY 20

ELEMENT	MODALITY	ASSOCIATED HOUSE	PLANET
Earth	Fixed	2ND • Values	Venus

- Rules the throat, has a noteworthy voice
- Has a practical, realistic and grounded perspective
- Prefers to be surrounded by possessions
- Is tactile, oriented to touch and taste
- Has a stable, conservative and reliable character
- Is determined, persevering and tries to complete all tasks
- Is loyal and doesn't like sudden change
- Brings a strong, determined voice to any chaotic situation
- Likes to be in nature

Gemini

I THINK

GEMINI PEOPLE ARE THE DEFINITION OF what it means to be agile. They think on their feet, especially if you are chasing them! These are people who love a good challenge, as long as it is a mentally stimulating one. But oh how swift their exit is if they become bored. The solution is simple, keep them guessing. Either that or they will always have you scratching your head, asking, "What just happened?" It all happens so fast with Geminis that you have to prepare to keep up with them. Their ruling planet, Mercury, makes it so. In the changeable air sign that is Gemini, Mercury is extremely adaptable and this is an admirable trait. It keeps things interesting.

More importantly, Mercury is the planet that allows us to interpret life from the mind as opposed to from just the body. Consider the amazing change that happens when a baby transitions from making sounds to forming words. Marvel at how the mind translates symbols into concepts that change life's trajectory. For example, when school children are learning to read, there is an incandescent moment when C-A-T becomes a living, breathing, reality in the child's consciousness. This moment is perhaps one of the most significant in life, because in this moment a young mind can interpret various meanings in life independently from others in his environment. In some ways, she is free to begin to create her own understanding of reality.

This is the strength of Geminis. They change our world with their ability to interpret life in new and exciting ways. They talk, write, speak and exchange ideas and information in an ever flowing stream of mental consciousness. We would be lost without this fundamentally human gift. Certainly, Geminis can respond to whatever is thrown at them with lightening speed. The challenge with Gemini people is that Mercury can be rather slippery. They play tricks, their words can obfuscate the truth. It is at the very least interesting to note that the 45th president of the United States is a Gemini. One can only wonder how the term "fake news" became synonymous with this Mercury ruled man. However, what's clear is that the boundary between truth and what comedian Stephen Colbert hilariously termed "truthiness" was stretched very thin under his administration. It wasn't just the 45th president. His vice-president, his personal lawyer and his favorite rapper (a man named West) are all Geminis.

If that is concerning to you, it might be a relief to know that the super talented and versatile musician Prince was also born a Gemini. There is certainly no intent to provoke controversy here. It is enough to point out how fluid and adaptable Gemini people can be. Whether that quality is used for good or ill, seems to exist in the mind of the beholder. Or as the inimitable pianist, vocalist and jazz pioneer Thomas "Fats" Waller once proclaimed, "One never knows, do one!?"

GEMINI
MAY 21 – JUNE 20

ELEMENT	MODALITY	ASSOCIATED HOUSE	PLANET
Air	Mutable	3RD • Mind	Mercury

- Rules the lungs and nervous system
- Is verbally expressive and quick-witted
- Can seem to have dual (always changing) personalities
- Tends to be sociable, communicative and restless
- Likes all aspects of mental processing
- Is agile, inquisitive, and open minded

Cancer

I FEEL

PEOPLE BORN UNDER THE SIGN OF CANCER can handle any intense emotional situation. In fact, the more emotional the situation, the more capable the Cancer person will be. In such situations, they blossom before your eyes. Where just moments before you witnessed a quiet, unassuming person, in the face of some crises of charged emotions or suddenly threatening circumstances, Cancers come alive. They live to help other people feel safe. This gives them purpose. Ruled by the Moon, they understand people's feelings, no matter how volatile. Ask a Cancer to help analyze the latest data or calculate the formula of risk versus gain in your latest venture and watch their eyes glaze over. They will undoubtedly try to assist, but gradually their focus will shift and you will be left wondering if you said or did anything to offend them. How could such a seemingly warm and committed person just energetically leave the room? The answer is simple. Cancer people need someone or something to nurture. They don't want to dazzle you with their intellect, in the way that a Libra person would. No, they want to be, like the passionate voice of Aretha Franklin, "a bridge over troubled water."

When they care, Cancerians touch you at the softest place and make you remember what it felt like to be loved without judgment. Being ruled by the Moon makes them the natural mothers of the zodiac. They believe in feeding other people. It's a rare Cancer woman or man who cannot maneuver around the kitchen with ease. But more important than feeding people, they have a deep and abiding need to know that they are offering something that will feed the souls of those they love and care for.

The tricky part for Cancers is knowing just how much to give and when it is better to let people figure out their lives for themselves. It would not be wrong to consider that Cancers are overprotective about anything that concerns them. It could be their business, their marriage or their family, Cancer people will never simply let things flow. They have to guide and direct. They have such strong gut reactions to the nuances of anything that they are involved in, that they never doubt their intuition. They are rarely wrong in what they feel, even if nothing is ever said out loud around them. They instinctively sense the truth. They will consider and feel the situation out before acting. The old saying, "Fools rush in where wise men fear to tread," clearly was written about a Cancer. But, when they do go in, they will come with a feeling of care and concern that will make whoever they come in contact with know that they have been loved.

ELEMENT	MODALITY	ASSOCIATED HOUSE	PLANET
Water	Cardinal	4TH • Home	Moon

- Rules the chest, breast, and stomach
- Is deeply intuitive and sentimental
- Can be very emotional and sensitive
- Cares deeply about family, home, and all domestic matters
- Easily empathizes with other people's feelings, including their pain and suffering
- Tends to have cyclic mood swings
- Quick to help others who are in need

I SHINE

AS PROUD AS MOST LEO'S ARE, they carry themselves as if they have nothing to prove. This is because they already know who they are. And they know that if you don't know who they are, it will become clear to you soon enough. Leos have no need to covet what anyone else has. Instead of envy, their state of mind is usually one of confidence. A Leo will never pray to God asking to be or have something that someone else has. They will pray for their version of whatever it is that concerns them. If a Leo is a musician, he doesn't want to sound like anyone else, he enjoys his own sound, thank you very much! If she is a minister, the style of her presentation will never be an imitation of a more popular preacher's approach.

The Leo knows instinctively that they shine best by being themselves. They are like the Sun in late July or August. They have no idea that any other reality exists but what they are bringing to bear on any situation.

And being ruled by the Sun, yes, Leos often emanate light when they are involved in a project. They have a warmth and a focus that inspires awe. And just like the summer Sun, people love to come out and watch them shine! It's no coincidence that former president, Barack Obama, commanded audiences around the world with his regal Leo demeanor. Neither should it surprise anyone to learn that Mick Jagger, the front man of the Rolling Stones, one of rock's most enduring bands, is an anointed ambassador of the Leo Sun sign.

However, if you are not careful, you can get burned by Leo's empowering sense of self confidence. It's not that they are demanding in the way that a typical Scorpio is, Leo's can burn you by acting as if you don't exist. Their light can be so all consuming that they don't have time to even consider that you offer something valuable and worth acknowledging. But, to be fair, if they have demonstrated their competence, it was already clear to you that they are unmatched in their area of expertise anyway. It just would have been nice if your Leo friend or partner made you feel heard or seen. Nonetheless, Leos will captivate you with their sheer strength of will and their consistency. They are great leaders because they don't give up once they have a goal. Leos can rarely admit defeat because they know that they still have more energy to burn, more heat to bring that will surely result in their success. If you have any common sense and you have seen them in action, you won't bet against them!

ELEMENT	MODALITY	ASSOCIATED HOUSE	PLANET
Fire	Fixed	5TH • Creativity	Sun

- Rules the heart
- Is self-confident and a natural born leader
- Has a dramatic, creative, and dominant personality
- Is able to commit and be steadfast in working toward goals
- Has good skills
- Is often admired by many
- Has a warm, magnanimous disposition
- Is generous and loyal
- Is capable of uniting different groups of people and leading them
- May tend to neglect the needs of others in their orbit

Virgo

I CRITIQUE

VIRGOS MAY NOT BE ABLE TO fix every problem, but you can bet your last dollar that they will identify what the problems are. This is the Mercury ruled sign that is focused on practical matters. In Gemini, Mercury is interested in ideas for the sake of nothing more than curiosity. But as the ruler of Virgo, Mercury must find ways to be useful, efficient and reliable. Virgo people always work hard to understand and master the details. It doesn't matter what field they are in, they will help make it an endeavor. Astrologers often assign non-glamorous jobs like accountant, researcher and healthcare worker to Virgos and no doubt, when one is in need of a professional in these fields, a Virgo will absolutely get the job done in superb fashion. However, we would do well to remember that there are people who dwell in the realms of creativity and entertainment, people who have nothing less than a spellbinding effect on others, who come from Virgo land as well.

Superstar Beyonce, and the greatest entertainer of the 20th century, Michael Jackson, are Virgos who are important because of the way their attention to detail makes everyone after them have to reevaluate their level of craftsmanship. Have you ever watched either of them move? Have you paid attention to the intricate level of spectacle that accompanies their work? Please, let's never relegate Virgos to essential worker category again. Clearly, these people can inspire.

Whether in health, science, or art, it really doesn't matter what the field, or whatever the sometimes irritating suggestion, Virgo people can make things run more smoothly and efficiently. It matters not if they are advising you on the proper amount of salt in your food, making sure you wash your hands for at least 20 seconds, or calculating the rate of amortization of your home mortgage, Virgos give a full scope perspective that you tend to not see and that will help you be a more effective human. They may not always be the most fun people to be around, only because their standards are so exacting.

Indeed, Virgos instinctively know that when given an assignment of any type, there are no excuses for not getting the job right. They have the intelligence and the skills to help you get precisely where you want to go.

VIRGO
AUGUST 23 – SEPTEMBER 22

ELEMENT	MODALITY	ASSOCIATED HOUSE	PLANET
Earth	Mutable	6TH • Habits	Mercury

- Rules the digestive system, particularly small intestines
- Attends to small details
- Prefers a lifestyle that is practical and well-organized
- Can be overly critical
- Can be a craftsman of the highest order
- Is service-oriented
- Tends to keep moving parts functioning efficiently

Libra
I BALANCE

LIBRA PEOPLE ARE RULED BY the planet Venus. It would be simple to assume that they are always filled with pleasing, cooperative and connecting energy, because of Venus' association with the idea of love. That would be a terrible mis -conception. Ask anyone who knows and loves a Libra, they will quickly tell you how difficult it can be to get along with them. They seem to swing on a pendulum, moving between extremes of thought and action. "What about Venus?" Well, it turns out that in the world of myths and in actual life, Venus is not simply a symbol of peace, light and everything nice. Venus is actually one of the most widely referenced deities of western mythology, most notably as the physical embodiment of love and sexuality. She has been cited as a goddess and as a sacred prostitute. Without judging here, it is clear that if they are influenced by Venus, then Libran people are complicated! Besides, who can be nice all the time anyway? That is an unfair burden to place on any sign.

The assignment that Librans are cosmically charged with is adapting in order to create balance and harmony out of chaos in the world. Their path is through balancing the dueling contrasts inside of themselves, especially their opposing, even warring, states of mind. Libra people do their best to make other people comfortable. Indeed they are gracious hosts and sparkling conversationalists. They can also be charming, romantic companions. However, they also have very strong desires that they struggle to contend with. Librans are challenged with learning to fulfill their own passions while also remaining connected with others. Sometimes this is a difficult balancing act. It's no wonder that in traditional astrology this sign is said to be in its "fall," or least favorable position.

The Sun as a force of nature is supposed to shine, not defer to other elements. Sun sign Leos understand this instinctively. They know that the Sun should simply be, without apology. But Librans have natures that are very much like the time of year in which they are born; not too hot, not to cold, always swinging somewhere in between. This is not a negative, as one of the wisest dictums man has ever received is the notion of "moderation in everything." Librans are always in some process of learning what that means. When they achieve that awareness, they become light bearers who blaze a path that makes it easier for others to navigate the proverbial slings and arrows of life.

Still, with all of the energy it takes to balance the competing forces operating in them, and however easy Venus' charms make it look from the outside, finding balance is not easy for them. The effort, the actual work of holding always impending chaos in balance, is what makes Libran's unique.

LIBRA
SEPTEMBER 23 – OCTOBER 22

ELEMENT	MODALITY	ASSOCIATED HOUSE	PLANET
Air	Cardinal	7TH • Relationships	Venus

- Rules the kidneys
- Needs peace and dislikes being alone
- Prefers to work in partnerships
- Needs balance and symmetry in their life
- Consistently seeks to be fair in all areas
- Will compromise to avoid conflict
- Sees situations from multiple perspectives
- Has a strong intellect and a creative mind
- Is inspired by good books, discussions and interesting people
- Tends to think through problems in dialogue with others

Scorpio

I REGENERATE

SCORPIO IS A SIGN THAT EXUDES power. Scorpio people are magnetic. Unlike an Aries, who shows up and takes center stage, Scorpio simply walks in and observes. They draw attention to themselves even though all they are doing is watching. The Scorpio is looking for a certain quality of experience. Often, the Scorpio person doesn't have a clear understanding to expect, but they know it when they feel it. If there is no emotional connection, a Scorpio will dismiss the moment entirely. They understand that people connect through energy that exchanges on subtle levels.

There is a misconception that Scorpios are consumed with sex. The misunderstanding is that it is not the physical act of sex, but rather, the emotional energy of bonding on a deep level that motivates them. Scorpios are emotional beings who desire connection at a deep level. The heightened emotional experience that they seek can be too much for people who are primarily mentally driven. Ironically, it is an intellectual connection that can lead to sexual encounters. This is because it is hard to articulate what is driving them. When they are given the opportunity to talk about what they feel they can be adventurous and open to discovering the new. When they find new ways of understanding how to release their emotions, they transform their lives, and then the lives of the people around them, in a way that can only be described as inspirational. Spiritual teacher Iyanla Vanzant has her Moon in Scorpio and through overcoming many crises in her own life, she has found a path to liberate others from their inner demons.

Scorpios often attempt to dominate other people. It is as if, not having conquered their own dark areas, they fear that those who they are close to will attempt to dominate them. Iconic jazz trumpeter Miles Davis was also born with a Scorpio Moon, and was often the subject of intense public scrutiny and fascination. People didn't understand how such an aloof man could make such astoundingly beautiful music. What appears to be the secretive part of Scorpio is actually a shield. Their intense thoughts and emotions trigger internal transformations that they are not able to articulate UNTIL they have a full understanding of themselves. In describing the power and fascination people had with his music, Miles Davis put it this way: "How can they expect to understand something in five minutes that has taken me

40 years to understand?" Many Scorpios find that there is an internal transformation that takes place for them in cycles each year. The exact nature of the transformation, while hard to explain, is a deep sense of awakening that drives the ambition and actions of a Scorpio. When those times come, they are able to show up as their authentic and emotionally connected selves.

SCORPIO

OCTOBER 23 – NOVEMBER 21

ELEMENT	**MODALITY**	**ASSOCIATED HOUSE**	**PLANET**
Water	Fixed	8TH • Shared Resources	Pluto

- Rules the reproductive system
- Is passionate and assertive
- Makes determined decisions
- Lives to experience intense emotions
- Keeps secrets
- Known for calm and cool behavior
- Understands the dark side of human nature
- Can be jealous and suspicious
- Can be ruthless and unforgiving when crossed

Sagittarius

I EXPLORE

PEOPLE BORN UNDER THE SIGN OF SAGITTARIUS only want two things in life: FREEDOM and the ability to explore and report back on what they have learned in their travels! Well, maybe there is a third thing: Sagittarius people often want you to understand how valuable the information they have gleaned is. As the teachers and philosophers of the zodiac, they honestly believe that their wisdom can help you. That's it. Everything else these people tell you is an excuse. They may work really hard, but they do it so that they can maintain their independence and travel. They may be generous and philanthropic, but they give so that you too can see something bigger.

The Archer believes that true knowledge comes from seeing the world. And the truth is, Sagittarians have always seen the bigger picture. These were the children who had to be threatened by their parents to come home by the time the street lights came on. They were explorers, rule breakers, even then. And even if they were put on punishment, as soon as they served their time they inevitably found themselves in trouble again; not because they are trouble makers, but because they are not fond of following rules and being told what to do. They do what they want to do!

Something in their nature simply will not let them sit still or stay in one place for too long. We should be grateful for their endless searching. Their souls guide us. My favorite Sag truth seeker of all is Maurice White, founder of the super group, Earth, Wind & Fire. His music and words epitomize the spirit of cultural leaders who believe in limitless possibility. You will have to forgive them if they also fail to show up on time or if they make a promise or two that they fail to keep. Their world is very busy and there is always some magic luring them to their next adventure. And they will tell you so in the most blunt way. These are not people who will try to finesse you with sweetness.

You may not see it, but for them it is just around the next bend of the road. How do they know this? Well, like their ruling planet Jupiter, Sagittarius people are visionaries. Perhaps they are able to see ahead because they just can't stand to look at what's right in front of them (they can be frustratingly naive), coupled with the fact that they are also impulsive. It may also be that the future looks bright to them because they expect it to be. This, no doubt, is their secret in life. They have learned by stumbling through life in an open hearted way, that positive intentions really do produce happy results. Why would they stop believing in a truth this big? Why would we hold grudges against them because they can't be bothered with seemingly little things? Trust. Learn. Live. Sagittarians understand on an inner soul level that living from their big hearts will always create great outcomes.

ELEMENT	MODALITY	ASSOCIATED HOUSE	PLANET
Fire	Mutable	9TH • Faith	Jupiter

- Rules the hips, thighs, and liver
- Is intensely curious and energetic
- Loves to travel and explore
- Is reliably optimistic
- Possesses a great sense of humor
- Needs a lot of freedom
- Can be tactless
- Loves to laugh and enjoys a wide diversity of life and culture
- Is philosophical and loves to share knowledge

Capricorn

CAPRICORN PEOPLE DON'T RECEIVE THE reverence that more extroverted signs like Leo do. Nor do they receive the type of whispered fascination that a sign like Scorpio is used to. The energy of Capricorn is hard working, extremely focused and dedicated to getting the job done. It is not the sexiest energy, but damn it, where would we be without people who can put their heads down and make something out of nothing? Capricorn is the goat that is pushing through challenges on the way to the top. It is an earth sign, but unlike Virgos who don't have a burning desire to be at the top of the mountain, Capricorns must. From an early age, Capricorn children learn to push through difficulty. It is natural for them to overcome. They are problem solvers on a mission. They are a life filled with boxes that get checked and awards that validate their strengths. Capricorns are also good at manifesting money!

But why? What drives Capricorns to such dizzying heights of achievement? And is this success what they really want or what they take on because of others' expectations? After all, Capricorn's ruling planet is Saturn and anyone familiar with traditional approaches to astrology will tell you that Saturn is not a planet that is normally associated with the word fun. Muhammed Ali was fun. But he pummeled people for a living. Hmm? Is there a way to see a side of Capricorn without having to be so serious? Well, yes and no. There's LeBron James, a sports hero and children's education advocate. There is Michelle Obama, a quintessential Capricorn with vision, focus, resilience, commitment, dedication, and a strong will.

The message should be getting clearer: If you want to get the job done with premium deliverables, you call on a Capricorn. There is definitely something fresh, exciting and beautiful about excellence.

Be prepared for the Cap to let their value be known in the process. Obviously they deserve it, what with everyone raving about everything the fire signs do. But a mature Cap does work that is motivated from the heart, not from what other people want or expect. Caps can be very serious and some have to learn how to have fun. But you will always know where they stand because they say what they mean and mean what they say. Still, some will even call them mean. The term Machiavellian can easily be applied to Capricorns who lose their heart and prey on others' weaknesses.

Overall they take their time to do things right. They know that time is their ally and they are smart enough to work with it, developing themselves and making the most of it.

In a world that is increasingly used to undeserved fame and robust fluff, there is no question that Capricorns break the mold. They are either working hard at something, examining it for its value, or turning away because it doesn't work and they don't have time for it.

CAPRICORN
DECEMBER 21 – JANUARY 20

ELEMENT	MODALITY	ASSOCIATED HOUSE	PLANET
Earth	Cardinal	10TH • Career	Saturn

- Rules the joints and skeletal system
- Is traditional and often serious by nature
- Tends to be a master of self-control
- Makes solid and realistic plans
- Has an ability to manage many people
- Rises to the top through experience and expertise
- Can be cold, distant and unforgiving

Aquarius
I KNOW

LETS FACE IT, AQUARIANS are usually very clear about what they know. They have thought about their respective fields of interest and they have found an approach to it that is unique. This is true even if other people don't agree. These people know what they know and they will stick to it, come what may. Aquarius is a fixed air sign. They came here to stabilize concepts.

Aquarians use deep reasoning and innovative approaches to address ideas that challenge the status quo and are ruled by the planet Uranus. The energy of Uranus is one of pushing boundaries by disassociation. That means that Aquarians are ruled by a planetary influence that asks them to consider whether they are acting according to a principle that moves them forward. Without that consideration, they are living a stagnant life. Whenever they feel things getting too stiff, they begin to break up old patterns and move in new directions. Of course, this quality of being is not universally revered. In fact, it can invoke real fear in people who prefer for things to remain the same. One of the challenges Aquarians face is accepting that sometimes they must let other people live in their seemingly old mental paradigms, even if it means that their advanced approaches are considered weird or eccentric. Still, it is clear that humanity is subject to forces that push us forward and pull us back. Aquarians are usually agents of the former group.

One of the most famous people in modern American culture is an Aquarian. She changed the expectation for what is considered good information, adding a swirling mix of spirituality and progressive approaches to raise the consciousness of every day people. She became so good at promoting a redesign of values and she resonated with so many people that she eventually became one of the handful of people known only by their first name: Oprah.

Decades before Oprah ascended to her daytime throne there, was another Aquarian who raised the bar of excellence and the expectations of what were possible so high that his accomplishments are still unmatched. In what is perhaps the most egalitarian sport, where the concept of leadership can change in an instant based on the circumstances in the moment, basketball legend Bill Russell revolutionized the game. There are many criteria that are bantered about concerning qualifications to be a GOAT, but one of the indisputable attributes is simple: the number of championships earned. By that account, it is not even questionable who the Authentic GOAT is: Bill Russell wins hands down. There are other important reasons for his revolutionary effect on his sport, and on the society in which he rose to prominence, that are beyond the scope of this book. What Bill Russell and other Aquarians give to humanity is a strong and determined mindset based on their belief of what is possible. Aquarian people live by precepts that engage what is known with what is possible to achieve, through having a strong and determined mindset. This is their gift to us all.

AQUARIUS
JANUARY 21 – FEBRUARY 18

ELEMENT	MODALITY	ASSOCIATED HOUSE	PLANET
Air	Fixed	11TH • Associations	Uranus

- Rules the ankles and circulatory system
- Has an intellectual orientation
- Likes to find innovative solutions to problems
- Has a need to be spend time alone
- Tends to be known as a progressive and humanist
- Can be objective and impersonal, seeming cold and insensitive to others

Pisces

I BELIEVE

THE SYMBOL FOR THE SIGN PISCES is a glyph of two fish swimming in opposite directions. This is a profoundly direct message that presents Pisces natives with a clear choice: swim with the flow of life and find satisfaction, or, swim against the current life and face dissolution and loss. The Pisces glyph is also a reminder that life is a challenge that will pull you in different directions, or in both directions at the same time, depending on your interpretation. The glyph symbolizes the private, inner self, in contrast to the outer, worldly self. Thematically, the Pisces represents the challenges of determining a belief system.

Pisces is ruled by Neptune, the planet that represents human longing for spiritual fusion with something bigger and more sacred than our normal everyday existence. It offers the promise of a mystical illumination. However, as promising as that may seem, the ruling planet of Pisces creates an imperative that natives born under this energy must always guard against being carried away to an emotional place from which they cannot find their way back. But the challenge to stay grounded lies precisely in the fact that Neptune always tempts those under its influence to search for something more satisfying. Neptune gives a very strong sense that there is something more to life than the mundane chores of work, taxes and death; and this sense is what constantly nags Pisceans. In a word, they are always involved in some process of soul searching. And to borrow a colloquial phrase, "the struggle is real."

Those Pisceans who have strong creative outlets often inspire the rest of us to believe that there is a magic in life. Whether they be poets, storytellers, actors, painters or musicians, creatives give us refuge from the demands of our everyday reality. Of course, psychologists, counselors, politicians, scientists, religious leaders and spiritual gurus offer all manner of refuge to humanity as well. Pisces people may embody any or all of these roles. While none of these occupations is a final resting place, they can temporarily act as a salve for the soul that needs to believe in something.

But how sad it must be for those Pisces people who can't find something to believe in, or worse, can't make sense of the messages they are receiving from the universe. Many of them occupy these roles as well. These are lost ones, who end up on the streets or locked away in correctional institutions. Perhaps we need a more enlightened approach to dealing with those who, whether through addiction or another kind of psychological collapse, can't find their way back to reality.

The highest consciousness of Pisces is reflected by those who see no distinction, no division amongst humanity. Quincy Jones, one of the greatest music arrangers and producers ever, is a Piscean who broke through many cultural and creative barriers to demonstrate that indeed we are united by a common legacy. His commitment to human understanding and celebration, especially through the arts, is a multi generational effort that has connected people from all walks of life. His signature effort, intended to provide relief to starving people, was a gathering of the then top performing artists from the U.S., sharing a glimpse of a yet unrealized truth, that there is a force that invites us all to surrender our false identifications and which affirms the fact that "We Are The World," a true Pisces message for the ages.

ELEMENT	**MODALITY**	**ASSOCIATED HOUSE**	**PLANET**
Water	Mutable	12TH Spirituality	Neptune

- Rules the feet and lymphatic system
- Is compassionate and caring
- Has an intuitive understanding of life's cycles
- Tends to be known for their emotional wisdom and spirituality
- Can feel like a martyr
- Is rarely judgmental and always forgiving
- Can become lost in delusions and addictive behaviors

Part II

THE PLANETS

THE PLANETS

The Sun and Moon are not technically planets, but for our purposes all the celestial bodies will be referred to in this way. As noted previously, all planets represent psychological drives that motivate us to act in very defined ways. Venus, for example, will always be the energy that leads you to find relationship with others. Mars will always be the energy that leads you to assert yourself. Mercury will always be the energy that defines the way you process learning and communicating. The style with which you act on these motivations is determined by the sign that each planet occupies. There are endless combinations of planets in signs (and houses). No two charts will have the same

issues to unravel. However, the planets that have the most powerful impact will always be the Sun and the Moon. Wherever these two luminaries reside in your chart, by sign and house, is where the central focus of your life's energy will be. There is so much to be gained by studying the positions of the Sun and Moon in any chart, because they represent the issues and concerns that you identify with most (Sun) and the feelings that you always return to as your base way of being (Moon). This cannot be overstated.

Here are a few examples. If your Sun is in an air sign and your Moon is in water, you will always have to balance logic with empathy. If you are close to someone who has a fire Sun sign and an earth Moon, they will always need to have practical security concerns resolved before they will ever be comfortable taking the kind of risks that are normally associated with fire signs. By contrast, anyone with their Sun and Moon in the same element will be a text book description of the qualities that energy describes. All of these examples highlight the reality that everyone has a different energy make up. But, if you understand the Sun and Moon placements of any person, you will have the keys to understanding the heart and soul motivations that every other factor in the birth chart will be filtered through.

THE PLANETS:

Answer the question "What"? What psychological drive is operating?

Embodies the energy of a specific sign in the zodiac.

INNER PLANETS

(Sun, Moon, Mercury, Mars and Venus) define your personality traits.

OUTER PLANETS

(Jupiter, Saturn, Chiron, Uranus, Neptune and Pluto) define traits that reflect your social environment and circumstances.

☉ THE SUN

- Symbolizes your core identity and your innate sense of purpose
- Represents your sense of self, basic personality, and general preferences
- Governs the fire sign Leo, the vivacious, dynamic fire sign that exudes bravery and theatricality
- Takes approximately one month to transit a zodiac sign

☽ THE MOON

- Represents your innermost emotions, your private self
- Influences the quality of your family relationships, your home, and your relationship with your mother
- Governs the water sign Cancer, the sensitive, protective water sign that defines nurture, comfort, and security
- The fastest moving celestial body in the sky and takes approximately two and a half days to transit a zodiac sign

☿ MERCURY

- Influences communication
- Reflects logic and rationality
- Helps synthesize and process ideas
- Governs the air sign Gemini (output) and earth sign Virgo (input)
- Takes 13 or 14 days to transit a zodiac sign and goes retrograde three or four times per year

♀ VENUS

- Represents beauty, love, and relationship to money
- Reflects interest in art, culture, and relationships
- Guides your romantic sensibilities and reveals one's perception of and expression of love
- Governs the earth sign Taurus (physical) and air sign Libra (cerebral)
- Takes approximately four to five weeks to transit a zodiac sign and goes retrograde every 18 months

♂ MARS

- Symbolizes the will to act, raw energy, determination, and aggression
- Provides energy that fuels movement
- Reflects physical passion and drive for personal expression
- Governs Aries, the impulsive fire sign known for its high-octane vivacity
- Takes approximately six to seven weeks to transit a zodiac sign and goes retrograde every two years

♃ JUPITER

- Symbolizes ways of discovering meaning, philosophy, abundance, and spirituality
- Rules expansion, encouraging us to widen our scope and broaden our horizons through philosophy, spirituality, and education

- Governs Sagittarius, the adventurous fire sign known for its thrill-seeking disposition
- Takes approximately 12 to 13 months to transit a zodiac sign and goes retrograde each year for around 120 days

♄ SATURN

- Symbolizes hard work, professional achievements, and steadfast resilience
- Can be harsh and unemotional. Under a Saturnian influence, one learns through tough love and difficult challenges
- Mediates discipline, restraint, structure, systems and karma
- Governs the enterprising earth sign Capricorn, which is known for its tireless ambition
- Takes approximately two-and-a-half years to transit each zodiac sign and goes retrograde each year for approximately 140 days

♅ URANUS

- Promotes energetic revelations (including feelings and subliminal realizations) that quickly alter old or established patterns
- Brings sudden changes of life, awareness, and insight that raise your consciousness
- Governs the innovative air sign of Aquarius

- Initiates ideas and thoughts that manifest as increased need for independent action
- Prompts rebellion from what is considered conventional
- Contains inner power that enables you to break through psychological inertia, fears, ego defenses and resistance
- Mediates the energy that revolutionizes your way of being (in the area indicated in the chart)
- Uranus is the force that allows new growth to emerge
- Is a great liberator or awakener (only perceived that way if one is not afraid of change)

♆ NEPTUNE

- Gives the urge to be embraced by something that makes you feel totally absorbed
- Creates the compulsive desire to seek a feeling of connection with all that is
- Creates a deep thirst for immersion in a transcendent experience
- Creates a yearning to be a part of a bigger reality that dissolves the individual sense of isolation and "smallness"
- Engenders the aspiration toward what you believe is an ideal way of living
- Brings the possibility of inner spiritual revelation
- Can promote the crippling clinging to false, hurtful avenues of escape
- Encourages spiritual pursuit, or if negatively expressed,

encourages different forms of pathology, including addiction, separation anxiety, narcissism, projection, infantile regression

- Brings saintliness or sinfulness; madness or union with the divine
- Governs the mutable water sign of Pisces
- Takes 168 years for Neptune to travel around the 12 signs of the zodiac

♇ PLUTO

- Contains concentrated power—like that of an atomic bomb
- Brings the death of the old to make way for the new
- Mediates feelings of disintegration (deep insecurity) which may lead to a deeper clarification of one's feelings, attitudes and values
- Can lead to the elimination of psychological patterns that no longer serve a useful purpose
- Plutonian patterns can be so deeply entrenched that great transformation occurs in a person's life
- Represents both the need for change AND the power that will shatter old ways and enable the process of change and forward evolution
- Governs the fixed water sign Scorpio
- Takes 248 years for Pluto to orbit the 12 signs of the zodiac and its orbit is elliptical

⚷ CHIRON

- Mediates the energy of the wounded healer
- Triggers deep inner wounds so that we can heal them
- Is considered to be a bridge between the inner and outer planets
- Rules divination
- Takes the growth you have experienced under the influence of Pluto to a higher level
- Represents the place where unresolved pain forces you to seek spiritual understanding
- Orbit around the Sun takes 50 to 51 years, primarily cycling between Saturn and Uranus

Part III

THE HOUSES

THE HOUSES

The 12 houses of astrology are typically displayed as a wheel or on a circle-shaped chart. The house wheel (or chart) is not the same as the zodiac wheel. They are two distinct wheels. The zodiac wheel is based on the Sun's apparent annual rotation around planet Earth. The Wheel of Houses is based on Earth's 24-hour rotation around its axis. The 12 houses of astrology are not "energies" like the elements or planets. They do not color the expression of energies like the zodiac signs do. They are WHERE these energies are most likely to manifest. The houses are the fields of experience, not the experience themselves.

THE HOUSES

Each house is associated with a set of traits, beginning with the self-orientation of Aries/first house to the relationship-orientation of Libra/seventh house, through the spiritual orientation of Pisces/twelfth house, which is the house just prior to beginning again at Aries. Each successive house expands outward into society and beyond in a greater way. At the moment you were born, the planets were all in specific signs and houses. When your chart is interpreted, the outcome is the meaning of each planet, the house it's in, and the sign it's in, to map the obstacles or gifts you'll face in this lifetime.

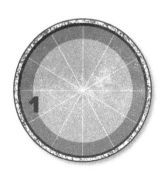

FIRST HOUSE

- The first house begins the zodiac wheel and covers all firsts:

  - Rising sign or ascendant
  - Fresh starts and beginnings
  - New initiatives
  - Leadership
  - The self and appearance
  - First impressions

- Cardinal Fire
- Ruled by Aries and Mars

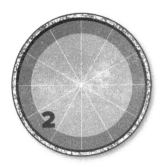

SECOND HOUSE

- The second house covers all matters related to your immediate material and physical senses:

  - Taste
  - Sound
  - Sight
  - Money
  - Smells
  - Touch
  - Income
  - Self-esteem

- Fixed Earth
- Ruled by Taurus and Venus

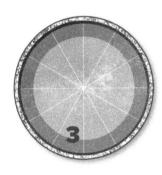

THIRD HOUSE

- The third house rules all forms of communication:

  - Talking
  - Thinking
  - Gadgets and devices
  - Siblings
  - Neighborhoods
  - Local travel
  - Libraries
  - Schools
  - Teachers
  - Community

- Mutable Air
- Ruled by Gemini and Mercury

FOURTH HOUSE

- Sits at the very bottom of the zodiac wheel and rules the deepest personal feelings about:

  - Home
  - Security
  - Children
  - Nurturing
  - Privacy
  - Parents (mother in particular)
  - Mothering abilities

- Cardinal Water
- Ruled by Cancer and the Moon

FIFTH HOUSE

- The house of what makes you unique. It is you, when you engage in:

  - Self-expression
  - Creativity
  - Attention
  - Fun
  - Drama
  - Color
  - Romance
  - Play

- Fixed Fire
- Ruled by Leo and the Sun

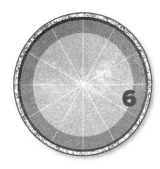

SIXTH HOUSE

- The sixth house is the domain of health and service. It governs our daily habits and how we function through:

  - Schedules
  - Routines
  - Diet
  - Helpfulness
  - Being of service to others
  - Organization
  - Fitness
  - Exercise
  - Natural and healthy living

- Mutable Earth
- Ruled by Virgo and Mercury

SEVENTH HOUSE

- The seventh house focuses on the way we relate to others, especially those we interact with intimately:

  - Companionship/partnerships
  - The alter ego
  - Business partnerships
  - Lawyers/mediators
  - Contracts
  - Competitors
  - Counselors

- Cardinal Air
- Ruled by Libra and Venus

EIGHTH HOUSE

- The eighth house is the house of transformation and inevitable change. It is where we are confronted with letting go in order to become part of something greater.:

  - Crisis/change
  - Death/rebirth
  - Regeneration
  - Addictions
  - Divorce/alimony/inheritance •

  - Sexuality/sex
  - Personal growth/ transformation
  - Partner's resources
  - Others' money/taxes

- Fixed Water
- Ruled by Scorpio and Pluto

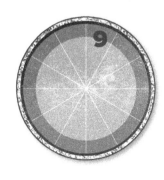

NINTH HOUSE

- The Ninth house rules all types of belief systems:

  - Sense of adventure/exploration
  - Religious beliefs
  - Higher education
  - Long distance travel
  - Publishing

  - Personal philosophy
  - Foreign language
  - Commerce •   Laws

- Mutable Fire
- Ruled by Sagittarius and Jupiter

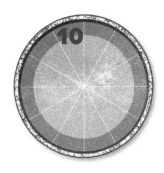

• TENTH HOUSE

- The tenth house is at the very top and most public part of the chart. It represents what we are known for in the world:

  - Career
  - Structure
  - Reputation
  - Masculinity/men/fathers
  - Fame
  - Long-term goals
  - Status
  - Public images
  - Experts

- Cardinal Earth
- Ruled by Capricorn and Saturn

ELEVENTH HOUSE

- The Eleventh House is where you make your contribution to society, and the reception you get there:

  - Teams/groups
  - Technology
  - Rebellion/Humanitarian causes
  - Friendships/society
  - Networking/social justice

- Fixed Air
- Ruled by Aquarius and Uranus

TWELFTH HOUSE

- The Twelfth house represents the freedom of the soul from the constraints of worldly attachments:
    - Final stages of a project/completions
    - The afterlife
    - Old age
    - Surrender to an ideal
    - Challenging emotions
    - Secrets
    - Separation from society (jails, institutions, hospitals)
    - Hidden agendas/secret enemies
- Mutable Water
- Ruled by Pisces and Neptune

REFLECTION

What more have you learned or discovered on your own about astrology?

Part IV

THE ASPECTS

THE ASPECTS

- An angle the planets make to each other in the horoscope
- Measured by angular distance in degrees and minutes (as viewed from Earth)
- Indicate the timing of experiences and events
- The more exact the aspect the more dominant it is in shaping your character

ASPECTS EXPLAINED

Aspects are relationships that the planets have to each other, in terms of proximity, that describe how they relate to each other. A simple way to understand aspects is to imagine the planets as guests at a party given by someone who has an eclectic group of friends. It's a wonder that they can all be in the same space together. Still, no matter their differences, there they are, for a brief time, sharing and absorbing each other's energy. Of course, some of these characters will get along famously, others not so much. Astrology uses the location of each house guest to determine how easy (or not) it will be for each to relate to others in the space. Some planets will be very close to each other and thus will not have a choice as to whether they will experience another's influence. Some will exist in such a way as to make it impossible to not see each other. Others will be moving in different directions and, through no fault of their own, will bump into each other and have friction. Aspects in astrology, through a precise mapping, a sort of GPS positioning of where in the structure of the space each participant is, can describe what the feeling tone, the vibe, of the planetary interactions will be. As well, aspects can pinpoint how these interactions can be handled in an open-minded way, so that the party can continue and be an overall success. There is math involved in these considerations, but in all cases remember, we are simply making sense of how planets are relating and reacting to each other in their various positions inside of a personal space!

Although there are many, we will describe the six primary aspects that are universally employed in astrology.

☌ CONJUNCTION

- 360° degrees undivided, (therefore, planets are 0° apart)
- Orb of up to 8° allowed
- Most powerful aspect
- Mutually intensifies the effect of each of the planets involved
- Favorable conjunctions involve the Sun, Venus and Jupiter
- Unfavorable conjunctions involve Mars and Saturn

⚯ OPPOSITION

- 360°/2 = 180° apart
- Orb of up to 5°-10° allowed
- Second most powerful aspect
- Balances opposite but related elements
- The planet's characteristics you accept are those you believe are consistent with your self-image
- Possible rejection of the planet that is less internally acceptable
- Lots of oppositions can make a person indecisive

△ TRINE

- 360°/3 = 120° apart
- A flowing aspect
- Easy and beneficial contact between planetary energies
- Planets share the same element: earth, water, fire or air
- Flow well together
- Reinforce and support each other
- Show what you enjoy and find aesthetically pleasing and spiritually uplifting
- Can show innate talents and what motivates you
- Enables you to accept your basic traits and accomplishments
- This is the energetic pattern where you fall back when things get difficult
- Too many trines show someone who takes the easy path

☐ SQUARE

- 360°/4 = 90° apart
- Occurs between incompatible elements, such as earth & fire, earth & water, water & fire, water & air
- Produces tension and strain
- The tension can spur action or make you grow
- Each planets' energies can get in the others' way
- Volatility of some planetary combinations can cause unexpected or spontaneous circumstances
- Can produce energy and impulsive action
- Managing the energy of a square gets easier as you age
- People without squares mature later (have not had to figure things out)

✳ SEXTILE

- 360°/6 = 60° apart
- A soft effect
- Occurs between different but compatible elements
- Gives the aptitude to do things represented but need a push
- Represents opportunity
- Number 6 represented by Venus (enjoyment and pleasure)
- Linked to rhythm/repetition (music)

⊼ INCONJUNCT/QUINCUNX

- Planets are 150° apart
- Planets don't understand each other
- Different element and modality
- Creates a reason to be flexible and compromise
- Perception of the energies of the two planets are separate and can be difficult to satisfy concurrently
- Requires continuous adjustment

REFLECTION

WHAT ARE YOUR FEELINGS ABOUT THE STUDY OF ASTROLOGY?

Right now, I am feeling...

I am thankful that...

I look forward to studying astrology...

I now think astrology...

Part V

PUTTING IT ALL TOGETHER

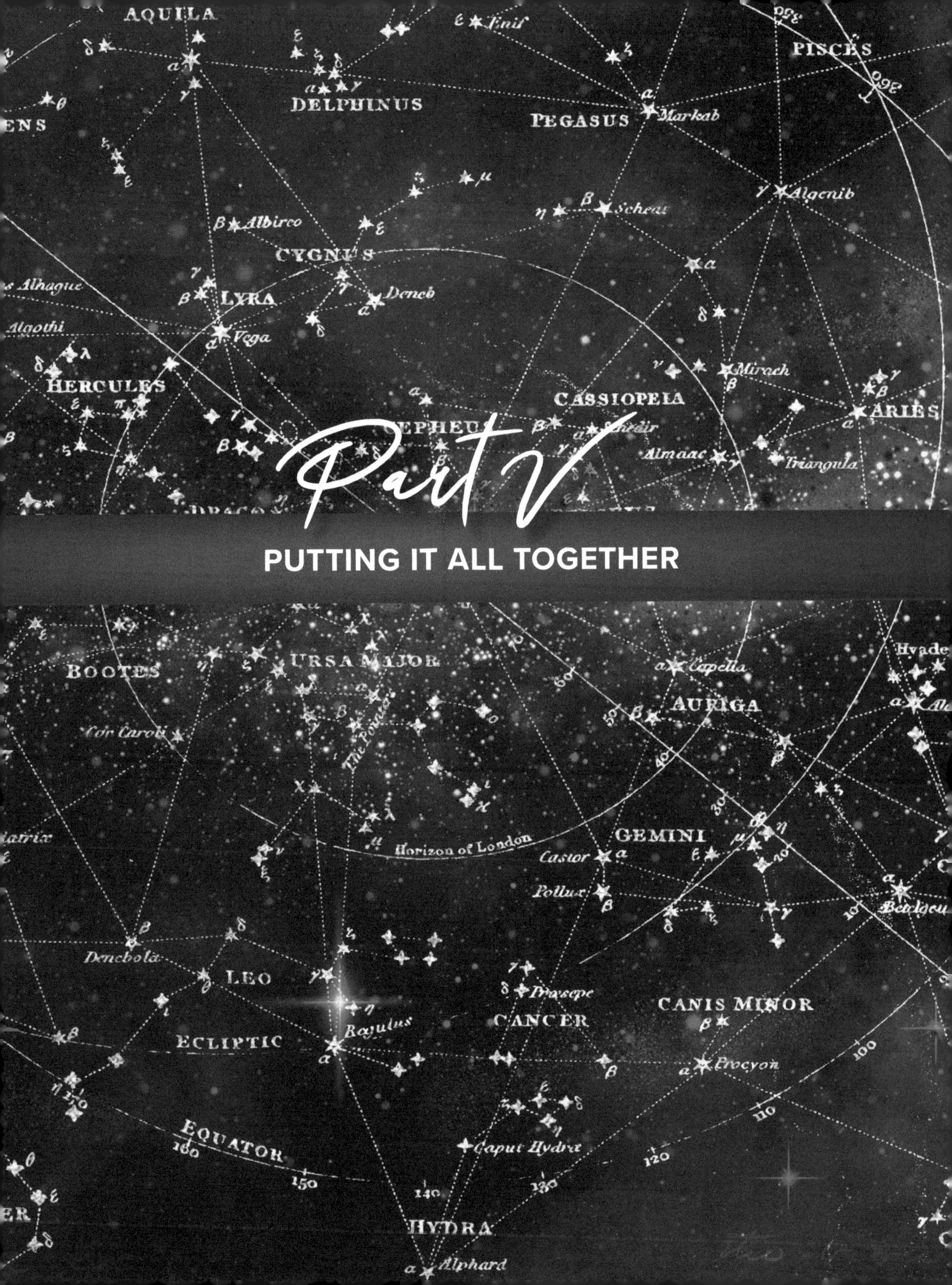

PUTTING IT ALL TOGETHER

ASTROLOGY contains

symbols that describe all human urges. These symbols work together to create a language of energy that expresses or manifests in time. Thus, astrology expresses both the character and the timing of experiences on Earth. Until you have thoroughly digested the material in this book, it will be helpful to have a simple guide to keep you focused. Use this short list:

- Planets show what psychological forces are operating
- Signs show how those energies are operating (their style)
- Houses show where (areas of life) planets are operating
- Aspects show whether planets energies will flow or not
- Every planet resides in a specific sign and a house
- Each chart has a unique combination of all the points above

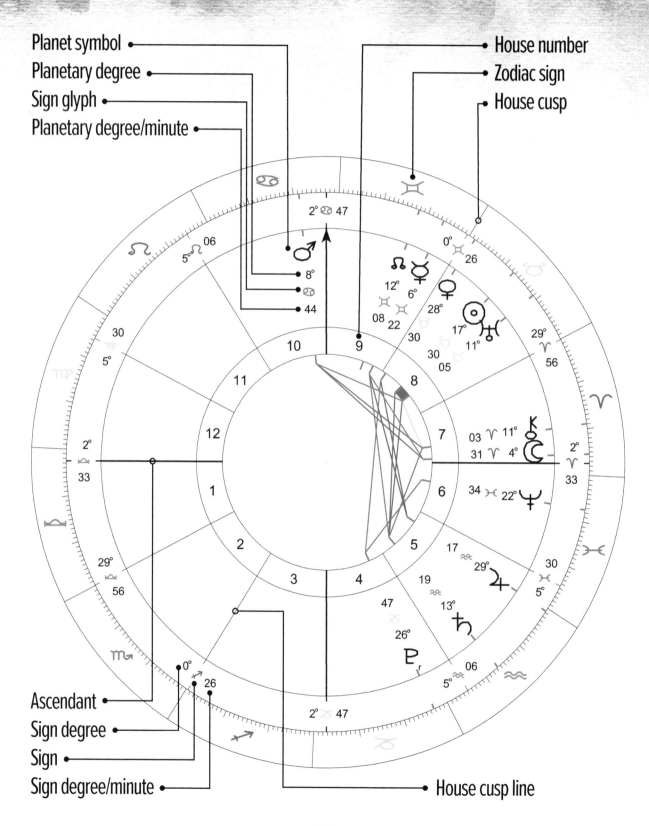

Planet symbol

Planetary degree

Sign glyph

Planetary degree/minute

House number

Zodiac sign

House cusp

Ascendant

Sign degree

Sign

Sign degree/minute

House cusp line

118

CHART INTERPRETATION OUTLINE

The sample chart on the previous page contains the symbols we have discussed in this book so far. There are planets occupying certain degrees in particular signs and placed in specific houses. The outline that follows will allow you to understand the fundamental energy that this chart describes.

1. Look at the sign and house placement of the Sun and Moon. Determine their element and their modality. The Sun is always who they are in the process of becoming. The Moon is always how they instinctively respond to life situations. The houses tell where their energy will be focused.

2. Look at the sign on the first house, the ascendant. This is how the person will present themselves, no matter what else is represented in the chart. Also examine the planet that rules the sign on the ascendant. This will add another layer of information about the person's way of presenting him/herself.

3. Look for the closest aspects (relationships) between planets, by numerical degrees. The aspects between planets will tell you how easily or not a person's different characteristics will work together.

In the sample chart, the Sun is in the sign of Taurus at 17 degrees, in the 8th house. This person's core identity is as a fixed (modality) earth sign (element). Read the Taurus section of the chapter on the signs and use that as a basis for understanding this person's leading characteristics. Do the same thing with the Moon, but know that instead of describing the core identity, the Moon in any sign will symbolize the persons instinctive habits. In this case, the Moon is in the sign of Aries, in the 7th house; which is a cardinal (modality) fire sign (element). The ascendant of this chart is Libra; a cardinal air sign, ruled by Venus. In this beginning stage of interpreting, understanding these 'big three' chart factors will tell you so much detail about the person's temperament, motivation and areas of life focus. What is the balance (or contrast) of elements? What is the leading mode of operating in life? Is this a fiery person? Is this a fixed, stubborn person, or both? Does this person react with compassion, or practical cautiousness? And no matter how they really are, what does Libra on the ascendant say about the way this person will show up and present? The easy part is determining the different types of energy a person is made of. The challenge lies in understanding how those combined energies all express through one person! But this is a challenge that will never bore you, because there is never a static, common answer! You must examine, listen and learn; then repeat. Every single person is different. The more charts you examine, the more the mysteries of human consciousness will be revealed to you. In some ways, the dimensions of experience that the astrological system symbolizes appear disturbingly complex. But in reality, they are simple archetypes that are contained in every soul. The important point is that the astrological system is a language that describes energies that you can observe, experience, and express. In fact, the only reason we know that we can ascribe certain qualities to individuals, groups and entities, is because we can see them acted out with our own eyes—and we can define them with astrology.

This is not a mysterious science when it comes to evidence. The mystery and art, the joy and profound challenge of astrology lies in understanding and defining motivations, the "why" factor, of observable actions. It is a way of understanding life itself.

Some of the most important research in astrology must be done in relation to your own birth chart and those of close family and friends —so that you can see the hand of astrology at work. The only reason there exists such a curious thing as an astrologer is that those are the people who have seen the system work; and they have cared and dared to look deeper so that they can explain it to others.

You are beginning the journey of a lifetime by taking your first steps here, where all fundamental astrological factors are introduced and outlined. You may wish to continue to more advanced studies. Or, you may wish to use the basic understanding you have gained to better understand your core motivations. This book will be perfect for you either way. No matter what, I hope this information will inspire you.

ASTRO-LOGIC

ABOUT THE AUTHOR

Lorenzo brings over three decades of astrology experience to help make the celestial influences clear. As testified by the clients he serves, his readings are accurate and shared in a friendly and caring manner. Conversations with clients surface specific and insightful information, insights about inner motivations and potential that client's can apply to their lives in practical ways.

Lorenzo's calling to music has informed his study of astrology; his experience as a musician and composer enables him to explain clients' life experiences and challenges in unique ways. For him, interpreting messages from the planets is similar to understanding patterns in music—whether a note or a planet—each specific element has meaning only in relation to the ones that surround it.

Astrology and music are languages that measure and interpret deeply felt frequencies. This is where having both intuitive and studied understanding of the rhythm and cycles of the planets gives Lorenzo mastery that benefits his clients. Just as he does with music, he is able to translate planetary language and create logic from their vibrational energy.

Lorenzo Sanford's mission is to share knowledge of these universal energies and to inspire higher consciousness. Through his expansive and integrated approach, he translates larger concepts into practical guidance that brings clarity to his client's lives.

Lorenzo is the father of Karla and Loren, two brilliant, brave and beautiful daughters who inspire him to be a better person each day. He lives sublimely on a lovely body of water with his wife Dorian and cats Ella Fitzgerald and Nina Simone.

ASTRO·LOGIC

AQUARIUS · CAPRICORNUS · SAGITTARIUS · SCORPIO · LIBRA · VIRGO · LEO · CANCER · GEMINI · TAURUS · ARIES · PISCES

Pan · Nephte · Hanumat · Typhon · Canopus · Omphea · Ichthon seu Dagon · Isis · Hercules et Apollo · Herenubis · Apis · Osiris · Ibis · Hammon

AstroLogic

CPSIA information can be obtained
at www.ICGtesting.com
Printed in the USA
BVHW021546130821
614294BV00023B/132